Locator Code: SFBC03

KEX0281253

Title: Uttering Her Name

Condition: Used - Very Good

ISBN: 9781907056192

Special Comments: 8vo   Some light shelfwear
otherwise a good copy

Shipment Tracking Id: 672

Entered By: Conor Kenny

KEX0281253

Uttering Her Name

GABRIEL ROSENSTOCK

salmonpoetry

Published in 2009 by
Salmon Poetry
Cliffs of Moher, County Clare, Ireland
Website: www.salmonpoetry.com
Email: info@salmonpoetry.com

ISBN 978-1-907056-19-2

Cover photograph: Ron Rosenstock
Cover Design & Typesetting: Siobhán Hutson
Printed in England by imprint*digital*.net

Acknowledgements

A number of these poems first appeared on the website of Poetry Chaikhana – www.poetry-chaikhana.com.

1

Dar Óma
    what speeded them on their way?
      what distances did they travel?
        the sky was full of falling stars ...
          You draw down too much light –
            soon the heavens will all be bare

2

Dar Óma
yesterday
I went looking
for You
and found You
everywhere
particularly
in the flight of swallows
                    innumerable
in the darkening air
it seemed they wished
to fan the dying sun
to flame

3

Dar Óma
look at this full fruit
falling for You every time
unconsciously

this tree
its limbs Yours
oozing sap
    its roots

its perfume Yours

lichen clings to bark
    hold me

deep deep down You are always there
awaiting my blossoming in You

kirtana of singing leaves

4

Dar Óma
holding Your image before me
on a screen
increasing percentages
until You disintegrate
like some forgotten galaxy
calling You back again
a retrieval
a respite from senseless oblivion

I know that stars are born
only to die
we see the light
of heavenly bodies
long since gone

this also I know:
Your light shines in me
the universe holds no terror

5

Dar Óma
You are not yet of my time
we do not eat together
sleep together
rise together

I will get up three hundred hours earlier
make toast in the middle of the night
smother it with honey

the moon will look in the window
curiously

out on the street
an urban fox
scavenging

his tail catching
the first light of dawn

6

Dar Óma
we walk the roads together
in the west of Ireland
Atlantic thoughts drowning our footfall

an otter
looks at us from a river
as though we were human

You relish the smell of turf-smoke
incensing sheep skulls

clouds borrow patterns
from fading Gaelic manuscripts

I pick forgotten fuchsia
fix it in Your hair

music wafts from a pub
distraught tin whistles

a crow alights awkwardly
on dishevelled thatch

I press Your invisible hand

7

Dar Óma
I became a night watchman for You
staying awake for hours on end
eyes peeled

once I almost nodded off
sensing You
I became alert again
scowling in the mirror
Tibetan mask

if I keep this up
they will surely honour me
with a gold watch

melted down
torqued
placed around Your neck

8

Dar Óma
I was a beggar
You threw me a smile

I ran off
delirious
into the distance

later, tired
hungry
I sat down

now people toss me coins

I throw them back at them

all I ever wanted
was Your smile

9

Dar Óma
I became a gypsy fiddler for You
and played all day
and through the willow-patterned night
long-forgotten tunes
of exile and longing
I grew a resin-white beard
forgot to eat
a seamstress fainted at the sight of me

I dashed off polkas
marches   slow airs
hymns I played as if they were jigs

wolves flowed down from the hills
and gamboled with children

I played to the moon and stars
to the wind and the rain I played
and the dead leaped from their graves
danced, and embraced

10

Dar Óma
out of aged cherry-wood
I carved a wind-harp
and placed it far
from the eyes
and ears of men
a hawk watches over it

no fingers touch
its delicate strings
the breeze it is
that plays the tune
breeze of morning
breeze of night
warm breeze from the south

throughout the day
it sings but You

wordlessly
effortlessly

never the same tune

11

Dar Óma
a day without those syllables
is not a day
mute twilight
    fog taking the hills
    in a loveless embrace
and wild geese
wedging north
no stars to guide them

12

Dar Óma
I wish to sculpt You

not in granite
You are not that hard

nor in marble
You are not that cold

in limestone
to absorb our tears

so as not to hurt You
I will chisel for just one minute
each day

wearing a blindfold
to protect Your modesty

13

Dar Óma
I have written a symphony for You
You should hear it
You probably never will
I'm having fierce trouble
with the orchestra

the triangle player
reminds me
rather sternly
that there are only three sides
to a triangle

the lead violinist shrieks
<you have notes here
that do not exist!>

I blush and stammer
<well, do the best you can ...>

<what do you mean softly?>
complains the cymbalist
<cymbals clash and that is that!>

oh, I don't know,
I fear it may never be heard
unless I perform it all on my own

14

Dar Óma
I come knocking at Your door
and say I'm here to check the –

mutter something

You let me in

will you be long? You ask

an eternity
I mumble under my breath
and begin probing walls
with a stethoscope

Your eyes grow large
what exactly do you think you're doing
You enquire, melodiously,
in a voice that will never die

I sigh something about trapped voices
in walls
prayers in the middle of the night
songs that nobody sings any more

I can hear something, I say,
a macaw, possibly,
but You are already on the phone

the police aren't all that bad
they allow me listen to prison walls
and grin when I recite aloud
    the lost sonnets of the damned

15

Dar Óma
I bought a two year old
and named the filly after You

my instructions to the jockey are clear:
<if she sweats up at the start
with excitement, dismount
rub her neck with sweet grass
talk to her
whisper to her
– try not to get mud
on those rose-white silks –
race her on the outside
away from the cheering crowd

move gently
rhythmically
be one with her

under no circumstances
shall you show her the whip –
and when she wins
by half the track
reward her
with this lump of sugar>

later, in the whinnying dark
I'll wash You and groom You
in the stable

16

Dar Óma
I was lying in bed
a moth came zooming through
an open window
and crawled down my skin
I couldn't move

Your light in me
had brought it in

17

Dar Óma
there are no woodpeckers in Ireland
(as far as I know)
I'd love to hear one now
rap-rap-rapping on a tree
as we tap Your mystery

herons we have, of course,
grey sadhus
experts in yoga
standing on one leg
little escapes their scrutiny

18

Dar Óma
find Yourself
a peasant farmer
to put food and drink
on Your table
bread to give strength to Your body
water to slake Your thirst
wine to bring cheer to Your eye

my bread is not for eating
my water is a wine
never meant for lips

let him sire a son
the babe shall have my name
I taste Your milk on my tongue

19

Dar Óma
I dreamt
I'd been to the ends of the earth
not to seek You
to avoid You
armed with talismans
I drew a circle with white chalk
a protection against Your smile
an inner circle with red chalk
against Your mouth
I gibbered in lost languages
the air was thick
with cabalistic formulae
then I heard You singing
shape-shifting
I became whiskered rat
You looked away
when You looked again
I was barn-owl
descending on rat
then I flew
for a day and a night
and came to a dark place
an even darker time
that time and place
before we met

20

Dar Óma
evenings darken earlier
where is Your light?
a murky mass of cloud —
an advance party —
invades the suburbs
a menacing horde
arrows of rain will fall
hastened by the wind
somewhere a candle is being lit
to a saint
who may never have existed
rumour added to tale
a folkloric mix of hope
and hallucination in time of plague

who now
and where
are seekers of light

    black rain

21

Dar Óma
the herring gull
repeatedly lifts a crab
carries it aloft
and drops it
on rocks below
until it is satisfied
the shell is truly shattered

the meat devoured
not a scrap left behind

You take me ever higher
clawing air
I forget my fate
submitting to Your hunger

22

Dar Óma
now
here
this minute
I cannot get nearer to You
or further away

the loon is known
to keep the same distance
between it and the birdwatcher

have You the loon in Your blood?

23

Dar Óma
when nobody is looking
I go snorkelling in frog ponds
marvel at myriad spawn

waving tails
unspeakable separations
before the miracle of legs

together we venture on to land
accomplished yogic flyers

reflected in Your eyes
a world of trees
valleys mountains
rising falling

sometimes utterly still

24

Dar Óma
snake unwinding
from a lightning–blasted tree
I've spotted You
why should I flee?
I am already deep in Your eyes
come
take all of me
mercifully
let me assist You
here's my head firmly in Your jaws
do not use Your fangs
to stun me
let me live
this death in You now
inch by slow inch

25

Dar Óma
many deities
and higher beings were jostling –
readers over my shoulder
waiting to hear
the next utterance
each in his and her own way
prompting me
helping me to find
a word-entrance
rhythm-entrance to Your heart
it was a veritable Babel I can tell You

in the end
I banished them to lonely towers
on high

composed and gathered in silence
with one finger
I typed out Your name

Dar Óma
I became a goatherd for You
searching for our lost goats
where can they be?
sometimes I think I see them
they turn out to be lichen-flecked rocks
men have been singing
such desperate songs for centuries

my herding is an old art
partly forgotten

I can no longer do it alone

You must come

let's pool our skills
listen and watch
I say, <no, Dar Óma
what You hear is a curlew>

 later You exclaim
<look! hoof-prints of a goat!>

You run ahead
the sun, low on the horizon,
strains to caress Your ankles
one last time –
am I chasing goats?

we rejoice
when we find the herd
we milk the white nanny together
in bonfire light
swapping teats playfully
milk in the bucket
splashes of whitish laughter

Dar Óma
after years of rigorous training
going from one master to another
breathing exercises
careful regulation of diet
avoiding loose women and strong liquor
I have finally qualified
as a basso profondo for You

last night was my debut
I sang the *Dar Óma Lieder*
like a deranged nightingale

  the audience showered me with flowers
I threw them back
<silence!> I bellowed, profoundly
(I could feel You in the hush)
<these flowers are for Her! for Her!
She who has crafted my voice

grab your staffs! your blackthorn sticks!
take your bouquets and posies
on pilgrimage to Her
place rose garlands around Her neck
and at Her feet
She is the source of your delirium
She it is that sings through me
wildly, melodiously,
the song of the seal in its lair
when tides are full>

28

Dar Óma
there is a candle burning
its white body diminishing

are You the flame
are You the body

must we both burn down
towards that final splutter
dedicating our lives
to that which licks no air
after we're gone

a candle burns
its white body diminishing

29

Dar Óma
I commissioned a weeping statue of You
and donated it to our cathedral
there are reports of miracles
the blind see
the deaf hear
the crippled walk again
most significantly of all
those in whom the rose of love
had withered
now weep with You

30

Dar Óma
I became an archaeologist
and discovered You
in fossils
ivy-clad ruins
combs   shards   bones

an old abbey
where poets lie buried
still dreaming of You
their unsung poems
in a dying language
sprouting all over the grounds
soothing dock
stinking hellebore
stinging nettle
dog-rose

31

Dar Óma
the cock
he crew early
from his midden
spreading Your beauty
across hill and valley

how steady he stands
arching his neck
the redness
of his vibrating comb
in the imminent dawn
uttering Your name

32

Dar Óma
I create silences
wherever I go
in silence You come to me
I close my eyes and ears
to worlds
my lips

if people ask for directions
I point to the gibbous moon
when asked how I am
I smile the cusp of an eclipse

should someone ask the time
they'll see in my eyes
it is Dar Óma time
to pray
and to praise

all of creation
is getting in the mood
insects flit silently
movement
but no rustle from trees
I cannot hear my heartbeat

in a distant land
You move noiselessly

sunlight briefly strokes the haggard face of a mountain
a hare cocks his ears
You listen

33

Dar Óma
I designed a gown for You
made of fish-skin
its scales glisten
when You wander out
among the stars

stars themselves wonder
at this reflected light:
what new galaxy is this
that outshines us?

troubled stars
they have just found out
their light is not eternal
disrobe!
cover Your body in ash
comfort them
in their vast sorrow

34

Dar Óma
I can never forget the yellowhammers
I saw as a child
tiny chicks nesting in a stone wall
such clamour from their throats
such hunger
nearby was a dark Protestant church
it was taboo to enter
God manifested that day in yellow
the colour I see You in now
dust of buttercups
primrose glance
You are the yellowhammer
ensconced in a mossy stone wall
we see each other
from different worlds
for the first time

35

Dar Óma
I am sending You a mute blackbird
with stories of the blackness of this world
war
starvation
death of hope
stroke his feathers
coax him to look into Your eyes
lay a finger
on his yellow beak
that he may sing again
that I may hear Your name once more

36

Dar Óma
following ancient steps –
Five Pecks of Rice –
I became a Daoist
and lay with a hundred concubines
at no stage did Your face
disappear from view
nor was Your silence shattered
by dove-moans or whale-breaths
never was any name on my lips
but Yours
no arms but Yours embraced me

37

Dar Óma
emerging from Your silence
Your chrysalis
what option do I have
but to fly back to You

that which touches
Your cheek now is me
that which goes in
and out Your window
is me

I am there
on Your pillow
at night
I penetrate Your dreaming
and non-dreaming state
I am the morning
witnessing
your eyelashes
as they open

38

Dar Óma
prepare to close this book a while
and leave it on the table
near some flowers
as I plan some other route
to Your being

the road so far was long
but seemed to only last a day
part of the night

You were my staff of hazel
my guide and companion
there was pain not seeing You
pain seeing You
I will read the lives of explorers
adventurers
imitate their courage and guile
faced by storms, pirates,
drought, deluge
unmapped territories
the knowledge that one is lost

I will go to sea as a Bedouin

Dar Óma
I went to the General Post Office
<I wish to see the boss> I said
he came, ceremoniously.
<You the boss?>
<Jaláluddin Rumi, at your service, sir>
<now, look here, Mr. Rumi,
can you send me by special delivery
right this minute to Montevideo?>
<impossible
you too fat!
anyway, post in Uruguay
something terrible
you might get lost … or stolen.>
I bawled my eyes out

he took pity on me
and did a whirl
You should have seen that Dervish dance

many hours later
he came out of his trance:
<go to Ephesus>, he said
<there you find a cave
and fall asleep for 187 years …>
that is where I am now
in awful slumber

Dar Óma
I went to my excellent physician
author of *Addiction Replacement Therapy*
he put me on heroin
and monitored my progress steadily
<is your need for Her
greater than your craving for the drug?>
I nodded, sagely

he put me on LSD
<what do you see?>
<blazing yellow harvest moons
orbiting one another
their beams are peacock feathers
showering on crab-apple trees
in the Isle of the Blest
their taste is dry>
<you don't see Her at all?>
<who else am I describing?>
the doctor is perplexed
the universe perplexed

41

Dar Óma
slowly like Venice
I am sinking
in Your beauty

Your grace
lapping at my door

when will I drown
in the spume-bright story of Your smile?

42

Dar Óma
tonight just one –
one swallow in a violet sky
is it pursuing insects
lost companions?
by its antics
neither –
back and forth
among the eaves
in ever-decreasing arcs
pursuing and fleeing its own cry

43

Dar Óma
the immensity of green
in trees, bushes, shrubs
convinces me
You are not heartless
    ward my feverish mind

majestic, wild One
You need me to water You
    with syllables

words pour upon You
moistening Your roots
    and mine

44

Dar Óma
look at the generations past
black and white photographs
of ambition, hope
simple decency
among them my betrayed mother
the only one among the children
wearing a necklace
like waifs
from Fatima or Knock
awaiting an apparition

I am my mother's child
my hands by my side
waiting for You to appear

45

Dar Óma
an infinite mass of cloud
pinkish from city lights
imperceptibly moving across
a waste of sky
fissured in unplumbable darkness
as though an ice age dawned
I thought not of Your beauty
I trembled at Your might
Your power throughout aeons
how easily You could crush me
in the blink of an eye

46

Dar Óma
setting out again in search of You
my ship flounders in Transylvania
how difficult it is to move
from You to you
     back again
wild horses of the will
rear as one
but there are out-of-work circus folk here
who promise to teach me
somersaulting
juggling
tight rope walking
all arts that serve to know You
and amuse You
come watch me breathe fire
the very flame of Your being

47

Dar Óma
today my heart is stone

a stone on a beach
You once walked
a long time ago

a sudden warmth
skin on the sole of Your foot

remembered more clearly
than sky
      ocean

walk, peaceful One
walk this shore again

48

Dar Óma
why was the veil rent
why did I ever see Your face
what madness
does my purpose hold

I bleed in my core

at least a stigmatist
has wounds to show

dark One, quickly,
send vultures

49

Dar Óma
rabid dog
bark somewhere else
in the netherworld
with Cerberus
glue Your savage eyes
to some other

snarling teeth
bristling fur
flea-bitten cocked ears
traitorous mangy cur
may You never be in heat

Beloved, who is it that speaks?
a dybbuk has lodged in my soul

50

Dar Óma
unbelievable
the grace showered on me
in my darkest hour
I didn't know above from below

were grace to fall
it would beat on closed casements

in crazy crystals it came
Your disembodied love

I no longer whimper
for Your touch

a tree of love is growing
I sit in its shade

the night sings
ghazals to the absent moon

51

Dar Óma
I have patented a talking rosary
when a bead is thumbed
it utters Your name
orders are coming in
from places I've never heard of
Athenians much prefer it to their worry beads
You inspire such creativity
 productivity generosity
already a free batch is hot on its way
to Ulan Bator
and other snowed-in parts of our globe
in need of Your warmth

52

Dar Óma
as I contemplate
a goldfish
suddenly it is You
such is the alchemy
of a blink
You rest
shimmering in devotion
how purified
the waters have become
how still

You swim in silver

53

Dar Óma
let me find You in a meadow
in that tart herb
we ate as children
sour sally we called it
find You in simple days
when hens roamed freely
scratching the earth

from elderberries I squeezed ink
imagining poems
I'd dedicate to You

I first discovered You
in a hen's egg
round   warm

I thought aloud:
the world could be like this
as it is now

Cloud Woman   was there ever a time
I did not hear You
promising to return
Star Woman invoked a million times
Long Grass Woman were You not always present
when I played and hid from enemies
Earth Woman that opens up when I'm gone

54

Dar Óma
the poplars erect
standing to attention
lining the road
mile after mile after mile
expectant
immaculately turned out
Your personal guard of honour

make Your appearance now
before one by one
they collapse in the heat

55

Dar Óma
a barefoot gypsy boy
with outstretched hand
repeats his begging mantra
softly
to the air
to You

56

Dar Óma
shade-giving vines
their grapes smaller
than those in the sun

I slowly ripen
in Your shadow

countless clusters of me
created in Your coolness

wordlessly hanging in mid air

Dar Óma
a clattering from a nearby canteen
they are preparing to feed an army

let me march for You
medals glistening in the Transylvanian sun

up and down I march
proclaiming Your freedom

I will defend You forever
against wasps
the devil's coach-horse
scorpions

a one-man army
watch me advance
and retreat

retreat
and advance
all day long

tonight
in the barracks
alone

I will plot new manoeuvres
tactics of ecstasy

tomorrow You'll wash my wounds
in the salt baths of Ocna

58

Dar Óma
up among lofty pines
crows are preening themselves for You

imagining themselves songsters
they praise Your name

flying with the grace of other birds
inwardly transformed

their crude nests
smoothed to a lovelier shape

hoarseness now a thing of the past
liquid their cry

59

Dar Óma
watching a troupe of whirling dervishes
from Damascus
one callow youth
    a spinning mushroom

what would our master
Mawlana say
        mushrooms
        pop up overnight
        nurtured by dung
something like that?

I want to write
mushroom metres for you
diction that springs
from my own corruption
words white
        revolving
            and still

60

Dar Óma
in a Transylvanian mud-bath
I cover myself in black
oily ooze
Ganesh smiles
mud cakes in the sun
an elephant grey

I lift You with my tusks
like a log far into the forest

all my past
spread out
laid bare

I trample on it
what else to do

carefully I let You down
You stand
where no one has stood before

the ivory silence
as You recline

61

Dar Óma
the museum of painted glass in Sibiel
images of the Wine-Christ
one of many vines that connects us
to our mystery

there are gravestones
some tilting sadly or humorously
an apple tree
begs me to taste of Your flesh

outside pensive geese
waiting to explode

I throw them the core of my being
they scamper after You

62

Dar Óma
I made a famous ewe's milk
cheese for You
they came from far
and near to view it
they came from Daia
rich in damsons
from Siura Mica of small roofs
Constanta on the Black Sea
imps – *strigoi* –
attempted to steal it
I uttered Your name
they scattered like starlings

63

Dar Óma
the distant clip-clop
of horses' hooves
rings out as applause
around the hills of Daia
slightly drunk on plum brandy
the long evening
stretches out to You

a stray dog glances at me
tomatoes ready to burst

I've been too long in the sun

wild flowers
penny candles
will burn at Your altar
when night
the gypsy with his knapsack
strolls down from the hills

64

Dar Óma
two storks in Harman
surveying the local scene
men and women
busily prepare the church
and grounds
for the Feast of the Assumption
vestments laid out
to take sun and air
wood, glass and fittings polished
to a shine
under the steady gaze of Michael and Gabriel

hedges trimmed
leaves and twigs gathered
to be burned
the village dead aching to give a hand

from their ancient observatory
two storks
supervising miracles

65

Dar Óma
I hobbled to Frasinei
for an exorcism
I switched from basso profondo
to falsetto
in the shake of a devil's tail
my demons were legion
the escape route traffic-jammed
half of You was still in me
I jerked
my eyes rolled

on the third night
my tongue fell down to my chin
then the rest of You poured out
like *The Wind that Shakes the Barley*
played backwards on a concertina
sweat ripples from the priests
lodges in their beards
turning to icicles
when I ask for my next appointment

Dar Óma
I could cut myself off
from the world of men
but not of crows
I cannot recall a time
not being of the crow nation

the way they fly alone
and assemble
their silence
 a disused well

in the distance
near at hand —
that's me
the one that's left behind

brazen in the morning
they rule evening time
painting their shadows on roofs

they hide
practise ventriloquism
expose tail feathers
say <here I am>

I try not to eavesdrop
on their intimate conversations
but am drawn in

Crow — You see —
battle cry, lullaby, lament,
subtleties of grammar, nuance,
Crow is my first language

Dar Óma
on a pilgrimage to the monastery of Simbata de Sus
for the Feast of the Assumption

the amputated
and broken in spirit
Orthodox nuns silent as sloes
bearded monks
Methuselahs holding each other up

scribbling on a scrap of paper
names of those in need of supplication
the living, the departed,
the undead

choral hymn-singing mingling
with cries of hucksters

icons kissed
over and over again

Your mouth must be dry

68

Dar Óma
if I had a cat
it would have that name
shadow
prowling the moontrodden garden

Egyptians shaved off their eyebrows
in mourning for cats

You slink away
come back to me
leaping
in savage love
scratching me in ancient frenzy

hearing You purr
between stanzas
as I read to You
in the small hours

soot falling down the chimney
with Your whole body You look
listening

69

Dar Óma
I have been practicing T'ien–shu
celestial writing
since early dawn
cloudy, weepy pictograms

all down the scroll
meaningless black tears

sullen rivulets
laden with detritus
long–lost being

I grab the brush once more
darker then bog–oak the clouds

my hand moves rapidly
scroll after scroll
one hundred shades of black

70

Dar Óma
I tried to become
a succulent Sufi for You
but look at me
daftest Daoist in Christendom
behold me performing *wu-ch'in-hsi*
first a tiger
    then a stag
        next a bear
            now a monkey
                finally a bird
flowing from one to the other
    in You
        tiger stalks You
            stag guards You
                bear taunts You
                    monkey makes You smile
                        bird trills Your freedom

71

Dar Óma
I am learning a magic dance
known as *Yu-pu*
first devised
when birds were observed
attempting to crack open pebbles

the steps come easy to me
all my life
I have been hopelessly trying
to get inside a pebble

I could have nibbled grain
breadcrumbs, seeds
as sensible birds do
but no
I've worn my beak away

constant pecking at pebbles
creates vibrations
turning the brain to jelly

beakless, brainless
would You have me in Your cage?

72

Dar Óma
happy the blood that sings in Your veins
warming me
happy the light in Your eyes
showing the way
happy the smile on Your face
sculpting these hymns
happy the heart
believing my words are woven
as a hammock for You only
sleep now
dream

73

Dar Óma
I went skiing
searching for You in snow
the air was thin
I kept my lips warm
by repeating Your name
to mountains and ravines

towards evening it began to snow
once-familiar landmarks dissolved

it has always been this way

I was born to lose my bearings

I should never venture out
my compass lies to me

I'll sit beside a winter fire
sweet-smelling wood Your aroma
flames Your ardour
Your hand rakes
ashes of despair

74

Dar Óma
I have been ordered
to sunny Montevideo as a spy
You will see me in hotel lobbies
engrossed in a newspaper
filling my pipe
whistling to myself
stopping at a florist
pretending I've a lover
inconspicuous in churches
museums
an innocent tourist
in light tweeds
a generous tipper in restaurants
while all the time creating secret profiles
of the citizens
their unrest
particularly Yours
You have been identified as a major threat
to stability, law and order
my mission is to kiss You
transferring a cyanide pill
to Your mouth

before our lips part
You will be in the hereafter
where I'll promptly join You

75

Dar Óma
speak to me
in Spanish
or English
I will translate automatically
into Irish
Navajo
Yiddish
I'm a Luftmensch
I specialize in air
the way it is forced
out of Your mouth
in vowels, consonants, sighs

I want to observe the curious behaviour
of Your tongue
moistening one corner of Your mouth
now the next
pressing against Your teeth
placed between Your teeth
the way You shape Your lips
guttural noises from Your throat

Your silence floods my being
an undertow carries me into the unknown

sea-monsters
give birth
in icy waters

76

Dar Óma
were You once Scáthach
warrior queen
mentor to heroes
fleeter than Your shadow
Your arm drawn back
Your gaze fearless
Your target visible in both eyes
with a cry
that comes from deep in Your belly
You release the spear
and before I have time to blink
beg for mercy, forgiveness
my rib cage is shattered
the tip of Your spear
hot in the crucible that moulded You
that holds You

77

Dar Óma
they have made me a member of their tribe
the last natives of Uruguay
what an honour it is
to serve You in this way

I feel 10,000 years old
and young again
there will be a great feast —
tapir, monkey, yams —
to which You are invited
I will paint Your body
with patterns from another world
You lie in Your hammock
under the layer of the anaconda
I take hallucinogenic snuff
exploring Your honeyed essence
vision after vision after vision
yowls and whoops the colour of parrots
in the forest night

78

Dar Óma
now it must be done alone
in the wilderness
without Your light
reflected in brackish waters

soughing winds
toss bedraggled rooks
this way, that way
at their whim
in purple gloom
reeds whisper to one another
inconsequential nothings
rats let loose on the world

79

Dar Óma
virgin mother whore
now hag
I meet on the road
don't point Your bony finger at me
keep Your scowl, Your evil eye
to Yourself
cover Yourself in Your shawl
be off on Your muttering way
back to Your mothball world
You have nothing to say to me
warm Your ulcerous shanks
at dying coals
leave me here looking out
looking in
tides ebb

80

Dar Óma
I've gone on walkabout for You
in the parched bush
already termites have hollowed out
a didjeridoo
I traverse a dreamscape
with You by my side
a lengthening shadow
not a kangaroo in sight
the vast emptiness of You
You allow me in
my pilgrim soul
You've known and treasured
long before Your first breath
bats are out
night's a whirr of wings

81

Dar Óma
if You were no more than a rat
on the treadmill
of my excitable brain
I would eject You
through every visible
and invisible orifice
but You are in all of me
somehow I inhaled You
absorbed You
ingested You
now I'm plagued

fire is the only remedy
for black death
burn me at the steak

don't look away –
earthly flames alone
will not consume me

82

Dar Óma
I have become a town crier
at midnight I commence
to call Your name
it is with sheer delight
that cats and mice stay up
to hear my bell
my unwavering voice
in sobering frost
some people curse me
from a height
many is the chamber pot
emptied on me
but I sing Your name
and soon they fall asleep
in each other's arms or alone
dreaming of You

I announce another dawn

83

Dar Óma
not a sparrow falls to earth ...
all things are known
in light
and cherished
let us know one another
cherish one another
grow in light

what of too much light
that sears
and blinds

once as boys we took a wasp
placed it under a magnifying glass
and –
how can I forget that execution
by light

forgive me
if I look for You in mossy shade
echoless leaf-strewn paths
turning over a stone or a log
slugs and beetles
all panic in the light
I take off with them
running for dear life

84

Dar Óma
You realize
there were thousands of other songs for You
all swallowed by a virus
in that process
which took less than a second
the virus became enlightened
spreading in all directions and none

cyberspace
is now awash in Your rosy glow
an Inuit shaman
recently back from the moon
tells me our planet hums
like the first ever aurora borealis

85

Dar Óma
meticulously studying
the barriers You place before me
from an engineering point of view
a military point of view
I am about to give up
when I chant to the one
who overcomes all obstacles
loudly I sing

Ganesha Sharanam, Sharanam Ganesha

I've taken the wrong route all along
hurried south to Your warmth
dallied north in Your coolness
looked east to Your dawning
listened to Your slumber in the deepest west
in all these madcap manoeuvres
I've been roasted and quick-frozen
opening and closing my eyes
like a tern I have circumnavigated the known world
You are not in any fixed point
how could You be
You are in the vibrations
of Your name
my name
eternal echoes of OM

86

Dar Óma
I'm a rollin' baba
rollin' down the road to You
a rollin' baba
all the way from Timbuktu
just can't help rollin'
can't think of nothin' else to do

I'm a rollin' baba
rollin' down the road to You
a rollin' baba
guess I'm feelin' kind of blue
just can't help rollin'
can't think of nothing else to do

I'm a rollin' baba
rollin' down the road to You
a rollin' baba
I really don't have a clue
just can't help rollin'
can't think of nothin' else to do

87

Dar Óma
cantering like giraffes
across an open plain
all things returning

nothing sinks
with the sun beyond the horizon
that does not rise again renewed
nothing is old
dead
or forgotten

momentarily unaware of their camouflage
feigned haughtiness
stilted otherworldliness
giraffes nibble green succulent leaves
in the brightest of bright mornings

88

Dar Óma
on first hearing its name
I wanted its shock
had I found an electric eel
I would have kept it close to me
jolted into awareness
whenever vagueness or revery set it

at the end of my fiftieth year
You appeared like an eel, a naga
from the depths

I bristle like a furry animal
sure of its doom
never so alive
as in the force of Your current
that moves and twists in me constantly
cell to delighted cell

89

Dar Óma
like Mira
chanting all day long
inseparable from her statuette of Krishna
the bee goes about its honest work
picking up Your scent
in meadow and field
studiously probing sweetness

wingéd gatherer of all that is good
hurry back to your golden hive
tell all your brothers and sisters
I have three more syllables for them to hum

90

Dar Óma
they desecrate it
who do not know You tread this earth
who do not hear Your anxious footfall
behind the screams of forest flames
now all the little crawling
hopping things of the jungle
in unison
utter Your name

they desecrate it
who do not know You tread this earth
who cannot sense behind electric saws
Your sudden intake of breath
now ancestral spirits
their voices ashen grey
in unison
utter Your name

91

Dar Óma
numbed by autumn
sheep stand
in drizzle
their fleece dull
in waning light

redeem us

utter Your name

non-migratory birds
bewildered on branches
longings
they cannot fathom

92

Dar Óma
You are why
I was born
to sing Your praise

You forge
the destiny
of my soul

Hammer me
into whatever shape
is pleasing to Your eye

The flames roar

93

Dar Óma
let us keep these miles
between us
sea and land
cool forest
hot desert
raging rivers
impassable mountains
gurgling swamps
all I long for
is Your grace

but this I have
in abundance
for what then do I yearn?
more?

grace is whole
and indivisible
knows no boundaries
obstacles

who is it I run to? who?
who is it I flee?
what hot forest is this?
what cool desert?

reach out Your hand
your warm cool hand
slowly I read your palm
searching for Your past

94

Dar Óma
looking too closely
at a vase of flowers
suddenly I saw Your skeleton
flesh ripped off
a grinning skull

why did I see You like that?

flower in death
death in flower

look how tenderly
I kiss those impenetrable hollows
where, until a second ago,
Your eyes shone

95

Dar Óma
my friends the spiders
are busy weaving
a gossamer veil

will You wear it
whenever I look
which is constantly?

not to see Your face
would be even more unbearable

spiders, stop
there is nothing we can do

96

Dar Óma
I designed a garden for You
built it with my bare hands
You should see it
flowers, shrubs, pathways, fountains, trees ...

of particular interest
to landscape artists and horticulturists
world wide –
the so-called Dar Óma Maze
impossible to find one's way out:
I nearly did, once,
and jumped back in again

Dar Óma
not the slaked thirst
of Bayazid
but the prayer of the Prophet
eternally on my lips:
more thirst

like a dog
my tongue hangs out

asleep or awake
how could it be different

I lick Your dew
from grass

howling
I create thunder storms

the air fills
with Your rain

long after it has ceased
trees drip
Your sound

I hear it
even when not listening

seeping
deeper than roots

98

Dar Óma
this morning I broke the world record
for deep-sea diving

You should have seen
the yellow, orange and blue shoals
expressing Your movement, silence and delight

but I continued downward
it grew darker
and ominously still
I thought I would implode

but then You placed Your lips on mine
I came up, gasping
for the air that is You

99

Dar Óma
seeking You in phenomena
like looking
for a corncrake
cuckoo
or pipit
You could be anywhere
I could be running around all day

I seek You
in Your silence
the silence You have opened up for me
let me be there
as silent as apple blossom
falling at Your feet

100

Dar Óma
in the beginning was Your name
unutterable
passion ignited in You
a hunger for dimensions
elements
galaxies
seasons

rumblings
leading to Babel
so that things animate and inanimate
might flourish in Your sound
die in Your light
and be reborn

grant me a life
closer to Your mystery
a salamander
staring from Your flames

101

Dar Óma
I'm in some kind of a desert
studying patterns
the sidewinder makes in the sand
I came here because Your presence
has caused untold havoc all around me
bus-drivers forgot their routes
street-cleaners began littering
all over the place – scraps of verse –
shops shut down for no apparent reason
alarm clocks went off in the middle of the night
the priest at Mass read Gibran instead of the Gospel
a fireman, awarded for bravery,
became a noted pyromaniac
well-known criminals took up yoga
indeed, an infamous heroin-dealer
known as the Cobra
is now into *para-bhakti*
and plays the flute like Krishna
a pharmaceutical company let all its white rabbits go
a back-street abortionist now sells organic vegetables
here in this desert hoping to see no signs
a sidewinder has doubled back on its tracks
how did it know how to spell Your name

102

Dar Óma
this bright night of the soul
harbours no dreams,
spectres,
no sounds

Stretching forever
it spells
Your name
invisibly
throughout the Milky Way
uttering Your name
        from uncreated stars

103

Dar Óma
I was a Papua New Guinean
wearing this enormous penis shield
when You arrived as a missionary in our highlands
You showed me a mirror
I laughed at myself
You laughed too
taking me by the hand
all the way from Genesis
to the Last Supper
then we ate and drank
before the Crucifixion

You admired my ornamental feathers
and asked me, finally,
did I want to be come a Christian
for You I would become anything
hang on a tree between two thieves
You immersed me in water
I was reborn in You

the very next morning
I showed You the bones of my unsmiling ancestors
one by one they perished not knowing You

104

Dar Óma
a faint aroma
of honeysuckle in the breeze

Can we draw a line
say here it stops
can go no further

Might it not pervade the universe
soon to reach Your nostrils?

Honeysuckle
fly to Her now with your sweetness

105

Dar Óma
I was a Prussian officer
whiskers much admired

Bearing impeccable
manners exquisite

Furthermore I was a crackshot
strategist
military historian
a what-not

Renowned collector of pistols
no horse
no woman
I could not tame

You spied on me
Mata Hari-like
and before I could click my heels
or bow
I was caught in your crossfire

In the course of I don't know
how many days or nights
(it's a blank)
You wrenched from me
every secret I ever had
all but one
and this will be revealed to You
in the silence of our next tryst

106

Dar Óma
through power of thought alone
I instructed a parrot
to utter Your name
which he did to good effect
but he was overheard
by my persecutors
put on the rack
his red and yellow feathers
plucked out
one
by
one
he wouldn't shut up
his last squawk on the gallows
Your precious name

107

Dar Óma
open your eyes
wide
hu
listen
hu hu
I am the wind
at Your temple gate
hu hu hu
a lost swan
hu hu hu hu
emerge from meditation
hu hu hu hu hu
wipe divine sleep from Your eyes
hu hu hu hu hu hu
awake
give ear to the last breath
of Your howling dervish
hu

108

Dar Óma
 winds sing the never-ending langour of Your limbs
canyons are tired of wailing
Your name in the night
to ghosts who come and go
seeking Your lips
to no avail

109

Dar Óma
the sun is in Your eyes.
No, how can that be
when You, alone, are the sun.
What creatures do You not warm
when I, lowliest of bipeds,
live only through Your Light?
The sun is in Your eyes.
No, that celestial body
has five thousand million years to go –
a flash –'a buffalo's breath in winter'.
Your body, however ...

110

Dar Óma
Your trickster, Your coyote
is called away
to Your vastness
an evaporation
far out at sea
beyond clouds
beyond stars
nothing surprises me

on earth have I not known
wild stretches of eternity
tenderly imprisoned
by eyelashes

release heaven
for the lonely
the dumb

am I being swallowed
or am I the swallower
a diamond-back rattler

release heaven
for the displaced
for criminals
sages
the beast in the field
the bard who dared
utter Your name

Epilogue

i

When I had a tongue
I named You:
    You gave me another tongue

When I had two eyes
I saw You in a thousand visions:
my third eye You opened

When I had ears
I heard Your thousand names:
now there are none

How good it is that You are everywhere
and nowhere

At last, at last
I am going nowhere
    You by my side

ii

There is no name for You now
nor is there form
in the now You are
not yet named
never again can I name You
am I not, too, the nameless one?

Index of Second Lines

About the Author

Gabriel Rosenstock is the author/translator of over one hundred books, including thirteen volumes of poetry in Irish. A member of Aosdána (the Irish Academy of Arts and Letters), he has given readings in Europe, the US, India, Australia, Japan and has been published in various leading international journals including *Akzente, Neue Rundschau*, and *die horen* (Germany), *Poetry* (Chicago) and *World Haiku Review*. He has given readings at major festivals, including Berlin, Vilenica and Medellín. His selected poems (from the Irish) have appeared in German, English and Hungarian.

He has translated into Irish the selected poems of, among others, Francisco X. Alarcón, Seamus Heaney, G. Grass, W M Roggeman, Said, Zhāng Ye, Michele Ranchetti, Michael Augustin, Peter Huchel, Georg Trakl, Georg Heym, H. Schertenleib, H. Domin, J P Tammen, Munir Nazi, G. Kunert, Michael Krüger, Muhammad Iqbal and his Irish-language versions of haiku masters Issa, Buson, Shiki, Santōka, J W Hackett and others are much loved in his native country. Rosenstock is the Irish language advisor for the poetry journal *THE SHOp*.

His *Selected Poems/ Rogha Dánta* (Cló Iar-Chonnachta) appeared in 2005 and the bilingual volume *Bliain an Bhandé/Year of the Goddess* came out in 2007 (Dedalus).

In 2009 he was awarded the Tamgha-I-Khidmat medal by the President of the Islamic Republic of Pakistan.

Uttering Her Name is his début volume in English.